Body Language

Communication Skills, Non Verbal Communication, Lying and Human Behavior

2nd Edition

Jeffery Dawson

Table of Contents

Introduction

Human beings are capable of feeling a sea of emotions; expressing them verbally is one of man's biggest gifts. However, not everything can be expressed with words. Certain things need a special language in order to be emoted.

That special language is known as body language.

Body language can be defined to be our body's natural and involuntary response to a particular situation or stimulus. This reaction is a minor change from your regular behavior and without trained eyes the change may be very difficult to register or interpret.

Body language is something that is universally prevalent and all human beings make use of it sometimes to express something that they cannot express verbally. The language is in fact prevalent even in the animal kingdom where animals use body language to understand and emote their thoughts and feelings.

Everyday we come across several gestures and signals that are used in connection with speech. But since everything has multiple meanings, how many of these gestures do we really read and understand correctly? How many of these gestures effectively help us read the other persons mind? And do we interpret them the way they are meant to be? Do we end up misconstruing half of them?

Well, let's find out.

In this book, we explore the meaning of the term "body language" and how you can use it to your advantage. We also shed light on some of the common gestures and how you can interpret and make use of them.

Learn how to communicate clearly and more importantly, learn how to spot a liar!

Chapter 1: Introduction To Body Language

Body language refers to the involuntary or voluntary expression of an emotion or thought, through physical behavior. Many times, we do not speak a word and yet end up conveying a message through our body language. It is essentially a culmination of several involuntary and voluntary body gestures that allow us to understand each other just by mere observation and without having to speak and listen.

We usually involuntarily convey our emotions and feelings through our body language as a reflex. For example, if you smell something rotten your first reaction is to crinkle your nose in disgust. Most of the times you do not even think about crinkling your nose and end up doing it even before you give it a second thought. Sometimes, you may voluntarily make a face or stick out your tongue to show your displeasure over the dirty smell.

See how effectively you communicated your annoyance about the smell without saying a word? This is how effective body language is. In this case, interpreting the body language was very easy and it was extremely simple to draw the conclusion as the situation and the corresponding response was pretty obvious.

A lot of times though, interpreting body language is not this easy. The art of body language has been studied for several years and many connotations have been arrived at. Despite studying body language for a while now, it can be concluded that body language is not an exact science. Various people have a different reaction in the same situation and the interpretation of the body language varies from person to person.

Bodily gestures are just as important as the activity of speaking and in fact, we emote 55% of our thoughts and feelings through body language alone. Our body language speaks volumes about us and a minor change in our behavior can set the tone of the conversation and set our image in the mind of the person we are interacting with.

Some of the various emotions that we emote through body language include excitement, anger, sadness, happiness, shame, content, relief, embarrassment and satisfaction.

One of the key aspects of reading the body language of an individual is to ensure that you know what the person is like normally, before studying their signs in a particular situation. One of the easiest ways to ensure that a person relaxed is to ask them a question that is completely unrelated to the purpose you have met for.

For example, if you are interviewing a prospective employee, he or she is bound to be nervous and this usually covers their usual behavior and makes it extremely difficult for you to get a reading off them. You can use this simple trick to ensure that the individual is relaxed. Start off by asking them a very random question, something completely unrelated to your purpose of meeting. Ask them about the people in their family or ask them about their high school or even crack a little joke about something random. This will ensure that they slowly relax and help you get a good reading off them, without the interference of their excessive stress.

Chapter 2: Why Is Non Verbal Communication So Important?

The way you look at a person, listen to what they say and how you react to everything the other person says or does speaks a lot to the other person. By just looking at you and observing you, the other person can understand whether you are paying attention to what they have to say or show and do you even care or not.

When something you say matches with the non-verbal signs that your body is giving off, the other person is able to trust you blindly and it helps create a healthy and long lasting bond between the two of you.

When your words do not match the body language signals your body is showing, it generates a feeling of mistrust in the other person. It also confuses the other person to no end. Should they believe your words or should they trust the signals your body is giving? If what your body is projecting is true, then why are you lying to them? This also results in the increase of tension between the two of you.

If you wish to become an extremely good communicator, it is extremely important to not only understand and interpret the non-verbal signals of the other person, but also learn to interpret and control your own body language signals.

Non-verbal communication plays five major roles in our lives:

1. **Repetition:** Non-verbally communicating using your body helps reinforce the idea you are trying to explain verbally. For example, if you are trying to verbally tell the other person that you like them, using body language cues like constantly touching your hair, maintaining eye contact, laughing loudly, etc. help reinforce this idea in the mind of the other person.

2. **Contradiction:** When you non-verbally communicate through your body language, sometimes you end up contradicting yourself. This usually happens when you do not believe in what you are saying or are lying. For example, you may be uttering the words "but I am not lying!" while you gave away that you are lying by not meeting the person's eyes or blinking too rapidly or staring too hard!

3. **Substitution:** Non-verbal body messages often can be used as a replacement for regular verbal communication. This usually occurs when a person cannot talk out loud or cannot express his feelings in words or is unable to talk out loud. For example, you wave out to people across the room when the room is too loud and you can't even hear your thoughts let alone your voice. Another example would be when people sitting in a lecture hall communicate by just using their eyes, by indicating at something with their eyes or rolling them.

4. **Complementing:** Non-verbal body language messages help add to a message by complementing them. This is similar to repetition, but this just adds to the idea, rather than reinforce it. For example, the boss may pat a person's back while praising him or her to add to the message and increase the impact that it has on the individual.

5. **Accenting:** Non-verbal body language messages may also help in emphasizing on a particular verbally spoken message. This is very similar to complementing and repetition, as the basic idea is the same: reinforcement of a particular idea with minute and minor changes. For example, while making a point, you may bang your fist on the table for an added impact, and make that particular statement stand out from the rest.

Chapter 3: Types of Body Language

Body language gestures can be voluntary or involuntary.

Voluntary body language

Voluntary body language refers to those bodily movements, like hand and feet gestures and facial expressions that are voluntarily administered by a person in order to convey a message. The person performing this type of a gesture has complete control over the gestures.

Voluntary gesture is also present among animals that react to a situation and express their thoughts through body language. Examples of voluntary body movements include smiling, clapping and waving hands to say hi.

Say you come across an acquaintance on the bus. You both have headphones in your ears and verbal interaction may not be possible. A mere smile is enough to convey your feelings of friendliness towards them, without making things awkward.

By clapping for someone you nonverbally imply that you liked what he or she did (in case of a performance) or are happy for them (in case of a happy situation, like a wedding or a birthday celebration). Implying so much, without trying to explain or express your feelings verbally. Similarly, it is extremely easy to wave out to a friend across the room at a noisy party than try to scream a hello! Waving expresses your emotions without you having to strain your tonsils.

Involuntary body language

Involuntary body gestures are those, which are not voluntarily administered by a person and are more or less triggered by the unconscious mind. A person mostly does not have a control over these gestures and these gestures are the result of a mental state.

Examples for this type of body language include face twitches and congenital mirror movements.

How you position your arms and legs talks a lot about your mood. The way you position your body speaks a lot about your thoughts and feelings. And of course, every minor twitch can be interpreted in a variety of ways!

Body gestures can be of the following types:

Posture

Body posture is an extremely crucial part of communication. Every body movement that we do and how we position our bodies can tell people of what is on our minds. It might be a hunched back or a restless leg, each posture signifies a different meaning.

We get into hundreds of body postures in a single day and they can range from simple ones such as sitting, squatting, kneeling and complex ones such as bending and stretching.

The way you hold yourself and the way you conduct yourself has a lot of weightage on what the person thinks of you. Holding your body too close to the person may give off the impression that you are too clingy, while holding yourself too away may be interpreted as you being too detached.

Facial expression

When we have a conversation with someone, our mouths are not the only things that move. We express through our eyes, our facial muscles and also our lips. For example, if we ask someone for a favor and we immediately bite the corner of our lower lip in anticipation of his or her response, then that also becomes part of our conversation that is emoted through body language.

Similarly, when we are talking to some we like, our whole face lights up. We cannot help but smile, and our face gets a reddish tinge due to the high amount of blushing.

Eye movements

They say that the eyes are the windows to the soul and the eyes indeed speak a lot about your intentions, thoughts and feelings.

Eye movements are voluntary as well as involuntary movements that people use to either make eye contact or prevent one or indicate something.

For example, when people try to show their gratitude then they look into the other person's eyes and display a smile and when someone lies, then they try not to make eye contact.

People also move their eyes to show discontent or disagreement by rolling it or move the eyes to point at something or someone.

Continuous eye contact is an indication of trust, whereas shifty eyes are an indication of a distrustful individual who should not be trusted at any cost.

Hand gestures

There are hundreds of hand gestures that can be voluntary or involuntary. Hand gestures in fact make for about 40% of our body language.

Animated hand gestures are an indication of excitement and happiness. It is also an indication of the person wanting your undivided attention.

Gestures can be further divided into positive and negative gestures.

Positive Body language

Positive body language includes those gestures that tell you if a person is attracted to you, interested in you, or likes you. These include gestures such as drawing in closer, making prolonged eye contact, sitting with uncrossed limbs, animated hand gestures, etc.

Negative body language

Negative body language consists of those gestures that tell you that a person is disinterested in you, dislikes you or is not attracted to you. The gestures include moving away from you, not making eye contact, sitting with crossed limbs etc.

There are simply hundreds and hundreds of body gestures and to list each one will easily consume several pages and a lot of time, and even then it won't cover them all. We, however, have tried our best to mention as many as possible and provide a short explanation for each in the following chapter.

Chapter 4: Improve Social Skills And Enhance Leadership Qualities

Body language can be used as an effective tool to improve a person's social skills and also enhance their leadership qualities.

Our body language talks a lot about who we are, even before we utter a word. Every little thing that we do with our body tells the observer about our state of mind. Just by observing for a few minutes, a person can judge us and understand if we are introverts, extroverts or lie somewhere in between.

Introverts are people who do not like to socialize and are generally of a very shy nature. Extroverts are the exact opposite and are extremely out-going and very confident of themselves. People who are partly introverts and partly extroverts display characteristics of both aspects.

People who are extroverts don't need much advice when it comes to improving social skills, but introverts need to be provided with the right advice to usher them towards becoming more friendly and sociable. People who display both characteristics need to strengthen their extrovert side and try and diminish their introvert side when attempting to interact socially.

Tips for Introverts

- Uncross your limbs

Crossing limbs the limbs means that you are not approachable and are always guarded. It is also an implication that you have no interest in the conversation taking place and that you would rather be somewhere else than be in that particular situation. It is also one of the most commonly observed traits by people while interacting with you. In order to attract people towards you, you have to keep your arms and legs open. You can also stretch them if they feel cramped but do not cross them in front of you.

- **Make more eye contact**

When you are in a social space, you have to make as much eye contact as possible. Maintaining eye contact is one of the main signs of interest and trust. When you dart your eyes around the room or keep staring at your feet, the other person get the impression that you are distracted, uninterested and are hiding something. Making eye contact allows the other person to understand that you are interested in them and attracted towards them.

- **Relax your shoulders**

Do not hunch your back and slouch. Similarly, do not sit up extremely stiffly, as though a drill sergeant has ordered you to do so. Relax and spread out your shoulder muscles. If you feel like they have stiffened, simply shake them to relax them.

- **Sit straight**

When you sit in a public space, always sit up straight and do not slouch. Slouching is probably the first thing that people notice and judge you as being introverts. When you slouch, you are implying that you are physically or mentally drained by the conversation and wish to be somewhere else. On the other hand, if you sit up too stiffly, you give off the impression of being uncomfortable. The person may also take it that they are making you feel uncomfortable and may just stop talking or doing what they were doing. So sit up straight, but like you have been punished!

- **Keep your hands free**

Keep your hands free and do not keep fidgeting. Do not constantly keep staring at your cell phone and keep your hands free and place them on your knees when you sit. Another bad habit people have is continuously glancing at their wristwatch. This implies that you are impatient, unhappy and are completely uninterested in the conversation. Constantly fidgeting with your clothes or belongings show that you are distracted and do not care about what the other person is saying or doing.

- **Laugh more**

Have a smiling face and laugh more often. People love other people who are jovial and spread a smile. Nobody likes a grouchy serious person. Laughing is an indication of interest and liking. Just make sure you do not smile too creepily or laugh too much, you will freak the other person out!

- **Look up**

When you sit or walk, always look upwards. Never stare at the floor and try to look at people's faces or look at something behind them. Look at them in the eye while talking to them. It shows confidence and encourages the other person to trust you.

- **Don't have sweaty palms**

Do not have sweaty palms especially when you shake hands. If you are normally a sweaty person, keep a hanky handy and keep wiping your hands on it. Sweaty hands are indicators of nervousness and that is not the first impression you want to leave on the other person.

- **Lean**

When someone tries to speak to you then lean in and don't ask them to speak louder. Your leaning in to pay attention will tell them that you are interested in what they are saying. If you lean away or ask them to talk louder, you are implying to the person that you do not care enough about what they say and if you miss what they say, you won't be bothered one bit!

- **Do not touch your face**

Do not keep touching your face. It shows that you are nervous. If you are sweaty the wipe your face thoroughly with a hanky and don't keep wiping every now and then. If you feel sweat dripping down your face, give it a quick wipe, but this should be limited to once every 10 minutes.

Chapter 5: Improving Leadership Qualities

What to do:

- When addressing a crowd or a group, take up space, do not stand in a corner and move around. Spread your weight and keep your feet apart while standing. This ensures that you stand up straight and exude an aura of confidence, enticing your audience and bewildering them by your confidence. When you move around, you ensure that you have the rapt attention of your audience. If you stand in one corner, it becomes easier for people to drift off and slowly stop hearing or paying attention to what you have to say.

- If you are showing a presentation and need to stand on the side, ensure that you have a spotlight on you. If that is not possible, keep a laser handy. In this way you can point to stuff on the presentation, without getting in the way. The laser ensures that you have the rapt attention of the audience, because everyone is always curious when you take the laser out!

- Place your hands on your sides and move them enough number of times especially while stressing on a point. When you animate your hands around, you ensure that you hold the complete, unwavering attention of your audience.

- You can also fold your hands behind your back, which will help your shoulders spread out and help you stand tall. Folding your hands behind your back also makes you look more trustable and it will make your audience respect you and easily trust you without hesitation.

- When you address a crowd or speak to a person, always maintain a consistent eye contact. Your eye contact will tell them that you are confident and that you mean business. Do not bury your eyes in your notes or stare at the floor. This will show your audience that you are not confident and it will make them drift away easily. One trick is to prepare cue cards with keywords and improvise on the spot. If you don't feel comfortable with improvising, thoroughly prepare your speech and keep the cue cards just for reference. This will help you maintain frequent eye contact with the audience, without sacrificing on your speech.

- Always sit straight and never slouch. Sit in a position where the top of your back makes contact with the back of the chair and your lower back doesn't touch the chair. As mentioned earlier, slouching is a sign of disinterest. When you slouch while up on the dais you indirectly give permission to your audience to slouch and lose interest too. When you sit straight, you indirectly imply that you mean business, hence gaining the undivided attention of your audience.

- Place your hands on the arms of the chair or place them on your lap. Do not place your hands on the table. The things placed on the table will easily distract you and you may start fidgeting with them subconsciously.

- When you listen to someone, tilt your head to one side so that you appear to be interested in what they are saying. Do not look down or keep your head completely straight. These are the signs of disinterest and may cause the person talking to you to feel uncomfortable, nervous and insulted.

- Consistently nod your head when someone is speaking so as to show interest. It also shows the person that you are listening to what they are saying and they are not talking to the walls.

- When you enter a room full of people look at some of their faces or straight in front of you. This shows that you respect your audience and directly connect with them. It also helps you gain the respect and the attention of the audience and it ensures that your audience pays attention to everything that you have to say.

- Walk slowly with even steps and not jog. When you walk too fast, you radiate nervousness and let everyone know that you are apprehensive about what is to come. When you take short, evenly spaced out steps, you let everyone in the vicinity know that you are confident and do not have a single ounce of jumpiness or shakiness in you.

- Use your hands to point, make shapes, clap, etc. This ensures that your audience pays attention to what you have to say and brings back the attention of those who have drifted away. How is this so? Usually while staring at stationary figure, we tend to zone out after continuously staring for a while. When there is a lot of movement, our brain tends to go into an overdrive and we tend to pay rapt attention. If you want to test this theory, try staring at a single, non moving spot on the wall for a while. After a few minutes you will notice that you start losing focus. On the other hand, stare at a moving object, for instance, the television. The moving pictures ensure that you have complete attention on the TV.

- When you shake another person's hand then do it with confidence. Do not put too much pressure so as to crush the other person's hand or give a limp handshake that will make you seem unconfident. The ideal handshake is firm, non sweaty and is just a touch and go. Do not hold on for too long or release too quickly. The ideal handshake is about 3 to 4 seconds long.

- If you want people to take you seriously, then simply roll up your sleeves. There is something about rolled up sleeves that shows confidence and makes the listener respect you even more. But, do not try this in an extremely formal setting, or else you will give off the impression of being disrespectful.

What not to do:

- Never stand with your hands on your hips as it signifies that you are over-confident and in a confrontational mood. It is a very informal gesture and will lead to the audience to lose all their respect for you.

- Don't walk around too fast or too much. Just walk up and down a few times and strategically plan as to when you will take your walk. Walking too much is an indication of nervousness. It also tires you out easily and results in a dry mouth, making talking comprehensively an extremely difficult task.

- Stand straight in front of the audience like Steve Jobs did and do not lean against something which will make you appear tired. Do not rest your weight on the podium or on the table. If you are tiring due to the continuous standing, go behind the podium and rest your arms on the podium. As your body is hidden behind the podium, you can relax it a bit without your audience getting to know.

- Do not look away or look down or up when you address a crowd or speak to a person. Also, do not stare a person down. Blink optimally and don't widen your eyes. The best way is to maintain eye contact with someone for a few seconds, shift your focus to someone else, look at them for a few seconds, and again shift your eyes. This ensures that you are not staring at one single person, making them uncomfortable, nor will you exude nervousness.

- If you wear glasses then do not look at people from above them. That might signify that you are not confident or sure of what you are saying. Do not look at people from under the glass either. It looks like you are looking down. Look through the glass at people - this exhibits confidence and surety.

- Do not check your watch too often, as your crowd will feel that you are not interested in addressing them. Rather, make sure that you never push your sleeve back to glance at your watch or check the time on your phone. If you feel you are running short of time or overshooting your time limit, make a joke about it and excuse yourself before checking your watch. This will show your audience that you respect them and care about their feelings, winning you major brownie points.

- Never place your hands inside your pockets as it will look like you are not confident in yourself and that is the last thing you want your audience to think about you. Instead, stand tall with your arms by your side.

- Do not sit with your shoulders slouching in. Slouching is a sign of lack of confidence and you do not want any member of our audience to have a negative view of you.

- Never cross your hands when you sit. It will signify that you are unapproachable and disinterested. When you are in a position of power, you need to be approachable and want your juniors to approach you with their queries and doubts. If you present them with an image of being unapproachable there will be a communication gap and it is you who will be at a loss in the end!

- Do not have a blank face when you are listening to someone. They will think of as not being interested. Have a pleasing and intriguing expression. Yes, this one is slightly different to achieve, especially if you are not even a bit interested in what the person has to say. In such situations, put yourself in the position of the person talking to you and think, "Would I like it if someone looked disinterested while I tried to engage them in a conversation?" When you get your answer, think about how you would like people to look at you when you speak and mimic that expression.

- Never look or stare at the floor when you enter a room full of people. This shows a blatant lack of confidence and some people may even interpret it to be a sign of deception. Walk in confidently, make eye contact and smile at people. This relaxes people and makes them feel comfortable in your presence. This increases their trust and confidence in you, making you rank higher in their eyes.

- Never clench your fists; it will look like you are angry at something. Rather, leave your hands loosely, form a loose fist or touch the tips of your thumb to the side of your index finger. When people look at your hands they should be able to see how relaxed you are, not how nervous you are by looking at your tightly clenched fists.

- Do not scratch your head or touch your nose of face in general when speaking. You will come across as being unsure of yourself. If you really do have an uncontrollable itch just lightly run your finger over it when you take pause from talking. Absolutely don't touch your face while talking, as it also distracts your audience from what you are saying and draws attention to the parts you are touching.

- Do not keep tapping on top of the table with your fingers; you will appear to be nervous or channeling anxiety. Instead, place your fingers flat on the table without moving them around too much. If needed, place your hand on top of the other and intertwine your fingers together in order to keep them from nervously tapping.

You can practice all the above tips and perfect them with time. It is important to not over think every action or movement, because then you will get confused and end up getting stuck between two different actions. For example, you may try to smile and enter a room, but end up smiling at the floor because you could only recall a part of the do's list.

Chapter 6: Microexpressions: Are They Lying?

Facial expressions are some of the most expressive of body gestures and give away what is on a person's mind. Even a slight change of expression can speak volumes about the person's personality, mood and nature within a split second. For example, if your girlfriend makes a face, even for a second, on the prospect of spending time with your friends, it can clue you in on how she is not interested in spending time with your friends and just wants to be with you alone.

Normal human beings cannot naturally hide every feeling and everything that prevails on their mind inevitably shows up on their face. There is very little you can do to prevent it unless you can pull off a very convincing poker face.

A poker face is the facial expression that poker players put on, so as to not let the opponent know of their actual thoughts and judge their hand. To pull off that kind of a face, a person needs to have complete control over his or her facial muscles and not allow anything to involuntarily give away actual thoughts. To pull off a convincing poker face the person needs to have an extreme control over their emotions and their facial expressions. This is an extremely difficult task and it takes years of practice to master.

A person can practice their poker face and try to be as emotionless as possible. Despite all the practice, there cannot be a 100% poker face since the facial muscles are wired to give away some little expression that a keen eye can easily notice away. For example, if you stub your toe against some furniture or get a paper cut or even burn yourself with some wax from the candle, you may try your hardest not to react, but due to the way our bodies are wired, you may end up slightly flinching or twitching your eye, despite trying your hardest to not to give away your pain.

Microexpressions

Microexpressions refer to the expressions that are so quick and minute that an untrained eye cannot even detect them. These can include a minor twitch, a minor tremble or even a slight tic that may be obvious to you, but may be complete noticeable to everyone, except for people who are extremely good observers.

Popularized by several TV shows, the concept has garnered a lot of interest among the youth.

Microexpressions can range from a series of facial movements to just a few depending on the state of the mind. The parts of the face that are mostly involved include the eyebrows, the lips, the eyes, cheeks and nose.

The expressions transition from active to inactive pretty quickly so as to not allow the opponent to interpret them on time.

The best way to educate yourself about micro-expressions is by reading about them in detail. Reading on the internet is the very best way to learn and there are several instructions and tutorials that are widely available for free.

You can also look at pictures and videos that will give you a better idea of how micro expressions work.

How to tell when someone is lying

Lying is an art that many people can master, but the art of catching a person's lie is quite a task. A person has to be very quick in observation and interpretation so as to effectively catch a person's lie. In fact, it is estimated that only 1% of people in the world can detect a lie without any prior training.

Microexpressions are the first thing that you should notice in order to catch a lie.

A person who lies will almost immediately bring the eyebrows closer that create a few wrinkles in the center of his or her forehead. This may sound like a very obvious observation, but the wrinkles on the forehead will appear and disappear in a matter of seconds, even before you get a chance to register the change. A lot of times, this happens within a span of few seconds, sometimes so quickly that you may not even realize there was a change, and you may think that maybe the change was a figment of your imagination.

When a person lies, he or she immediately starts to blink rapidly and avoids making eye contact. Another thing that the person will do is blink for a longer amount of time, which means that the person will prolong the blinking during and after speaking a lie. Some people may try to slow down their blinking while lying and end up blinking slower than usual. Even that is a sign of lying.

Also, when it comes to eye movement, a right-handed person who lies will immediately look up to the right. If the person looks to the left then it means that the person is only remembering something. The opposite applies to left-handed people. They may not turn their head in a particular direction; they may just avert their eyes in that particular direction.

While rolling the eyes, the person might also most likely place a finger over the lips with the tip sitting over the nose.

The Voice

When a person lies, he or she mostly speaks in a monotone or pauses a little in between the lie. Usually, the person will speak the lie in a single breath. Another thing about the voice is that they may even stutter or stop at certain places while speaking, where a pause wasn't necessary.

Observe the person after you feel like he or she is lying and if he or she drinks water to remedy a dry mouth. While lying, a person's mouth dries out owing to the tension, stress and anxiety. This doesn't mean that every person who drinks a glass of water after talking is a liar. Observe other signs too, and if they are coupled with regularly drinking water, you can be sure that the person is lying to you.

Distraction

A person who lies will be extremely interested in a different topic almost immediately. It is especially prominent if the person realizes that you might have caught them telling a lie. They will either themselves change the topic or start contributing to a topic that you pick up on even before you finish saying your sentence.

The person will be extremely eager to change the topic and get rid of the awkward situation created. Sometimes they may even contradict themselves and may try to distract you with another topic so that you do not pick up their faux pass. If you feel there is something weird about them abruptly changing the topic, they are probably lying.

Body language

A person might quickly join hands and interlock them and start massaging the interlocked thumb with the free thumb. As soon as you see that happening, quickly notice their face for a micro-expression to occur.

Ask point blank

As soon as they are done speaking, immediately ask them if they are telling you the truth. Most of the time, their cheeks will flush with blood and go red. They may also avert their eyes to anywhere but your face. They may stare at their own feet and even start grasping to get the correct words. A liar will almost immediately feel a rush of fear and guilt and admit to having lied.

It is important to note here that the above mentioned data may not hold true for all cases and cannot be fully and exclusively relied on as tests for lie detection. These are just the general signs of a person lying. Some people may be immune to displaying such signs, while others may display some completely different signs when they lie. It is only with repeated observation that you can realize which signs apply to the person under observation and what the signs are that they display when they lie. Once you observe an individual over a prolonged period of time, you will be able to catch the minor changes in their body language and catch heir lies almost immediately.

Chapter 7: Eleven Common Indicators Of A Liar

Apart from the aforementioned signs, these 11 indicators are the telltale signs of a liar. They may or may not apply to everyone, so it is better to study the person before coming to any conclusion.

1. They quickly change the position of their head.

When you ask someone o question or engage them in a conversation, observe their head and its movements. Do they retract their head or jerk it back? Do they bow their head or cock it up? Do they tilt their head? If they do any of the aforementioned things suddenly, as soon as you begin your statement or as soon as you end it, you can be sure that the answer to your question or statement will be a lie.

2. The way they breath changes immediately

Breathing extremely deeply is the most common reflex action when someone attempts to speak a lie. The most obvious change will be in the position of their shoulders. They will immediately rise and their voice will get shallower than their normal pitch.

This is because that when an individual lies, their heart rate shoots up and the blood flow also changes. This is because it evokes a feeling of nervousness and an individual starts to feel tensed up, resulting in deep and long breaths.

3. When they stand, they stand very still, without moving too much

Yes, fidgeting is normally associated with nervousness, but the people who remain in a still position and do not move around too much are the people to watch out for.

Why is it so, you ask? Well our mind has two primitive modes – fight or flight. Staying completely still is a "fight" response of the brain, as it prepares itself for a possible encounter. When you talk normally with any person, you tend to move your body about in extremely subtle ways, movements that are very relaxed in nature and mostly are unconscious. So, when something is off about the situation that you are in, you tend to get rigid and try to avoid any movement that will bring undue attention to yourself.

So, when someone goes rigid, it should ring all sorts of alarm bells in your head, because they may be lying to you!

4. They repeatedly use the same words and phrases over and over again

This phenomenon occurs because the person is trying to prove to you and assure themselves and you that what they are saying is the truth. It is like they are attempting to assure themselves that their lie is in fact a truth. For example they may keep repeating the words "I did not do it...I did not do it..."

Another reason why they repeating the same thing over and over again is so that they can get some extra time to pull their thoughts together and plan what to say next and how to convince you of their lies.

5. They provide unneeded extra information that was not required

Liars tend to talk a lot and provide you with a lot of extra information that was not required at all! This because they believe that the more they talk and the more information they give, the more believable their lie will be. Most of the time this information is absolutely not required and sometimes this information may be a bit too much in detail.

For example, they may tell you extra embarrassing stuff, totally unrelated to the topic, and you may end up wondering why they are providing you with so much extra unneeded information.

So, if they start giving you extra information, be assured that they are trying to distract you with the extra information and are lying to you!

6. They constantly keep touching their face or keep covering their mouth with their hand or a book or any other thing

One of the most common signs of lying is that the person who is lying will often put their hand on their mouth or hide their face and mouth behind something. This is because they wish to avoid the situation and want to ignore an impending issue or any question that you may have put in front of them.

When a person places their hand on their mouth, it is a clear indicator that they wish to hide something and are not revealing everything they know. The hand on the mouth is meant to be a literal closure of communication.

7. They will naturally cover and try to protect the vulnerable parts of their body

This includes areas like the chest, abdomen, throat or their nether regions.

People who are lying or trying to hide something will instinctively try to shield the vulnerable and exposed parts of their body by covering them using their arms or contorting their body in a way to cover those areas.

You may often notice that while talking, a person may place his hand on his or her throat and gently massage it, or bend low and grab their knees with their hands. These are sure indicators of lies.

This is because it is a primitive instinct inside us that demands the vulnerable areas of our body, in case our lie is discovered and the situation turns from talking to hand to hand fighting in a matter of minutes.

8. They keep moving their feet around

The shuffling of feet happens when our subconscious urge takes over our body. When an individual shuffles his or her feet, it shows that the person is nervous and is uncomfortable in his or her surroundings and the situation he or she are being subjected to.

This also shows that he or she wishes to walk away from the situation as soon as he or she can.

So, while talking to you, if a person starts moving their feet about, you know what to make of anything that they say or do.

9. Speaking becomes an extremely difficult task to do

If you want to know whether this is true or not, try watching a video of an interrogation of a possible suspect. You will notice that as time passes, it becomes more and more difficult for him or her to speak coherently.

This is because as reflex action, the nervous system reduces the flow of the saliva into the mouth when the body is under extreme stress. Due to the lack of saliva, the mucous membrane of the mouth dries out, making it extremely difficult to speak.

Some other signs you should look out for are pursed lips or biting of the lower lip. Both are thorough indicators of the person speaking a lie.

10. Blinking is reduced and they keep staring at you, often not blinking

Normally, when a person lies, they usually try to break eye contact with you. This is a very common sign of lying, easily recognizable by even the untrained. This is why, the liar may try to go the extra mile and try and maintain steady eye contact in order to gain your trust and show you that they are not lying.

But, in an attempt to come off as normal, they may maintain a longer eye contact, which is borderline staring, and may not blink as often as it is normal.

When an individual says the truth, he will often look away from the person, break eye contact every few seconds and look around. A liar will maintain a steady gaze without looking away.

Rapidly blinking is also a sign of lying. In order to keep their blinking steady and "normal", a liar will blink and often end up blinking at a rate that is faster than normal, giving away that they are lying.

11. They will usually play the blame game in order to divert the attention of them

A liar will often become extremely defensive or hostile in order to turn the tables on you. This is because they are angry and scared that you have or may discover that they are lying and accuse them. So, before you get a chance to blame or accuse them, they will point their fingers towards you and blame you for lying, whereas the situation is the other way around.

Trigger happy pointing fingers is one of the main signs of a scared liar who is worried that he will be caught soon if he doesn't do anything about it. They may also blame a third party not present in the situation in order to bid for time and come up with a better story in the meanwhile.

Chapter 8: Ten Tips To Keep In Mind For Stronger Body Language

Body language, as mentioned earlier, plays a very important role in communication. Effectively using body language to your advantage can do wonders to your social skills. These 10 tips will help you gain a powerful body language that exudes a strong persona even before you speak a word.

1. Get into a powerful pose to increase your confidence levels

According to the researchers at the Harvard Business School and the Columbia Business School, when you hold your body into a high power position for even two minutes, it results in higher levels of testosterone in your body and reduced levels of cortisol in the body. Higher levels of testosterone are linked to increase in the dominance and power, while lower levels of cortisol is linked to lower levels of stress in the body.

So what are these "high power" positions that have such a large impact on your body? These positions are any poses that make you feel powerful and in control of the situation. For example, placing your hands behind your head and propping your legs on a desk makes you feel like you are in a position of power. Also, standing with your legs spaced out and arms spread far apart make you feel as though you have complete power over your life.

So, the next time you are feeling low and hesitant, but want to present yourself as an extremely confident individual, try getting into a position of power few minutes before you need to present yourself. This position will cause not only a shift in the hormones in your body, but it will also lead to an increase of the feeling of being in power and makes you take risks that you may have normally avoided.

2. When you listen, people will speak more, resulting in increased participation

Do you really wish that there were more people participating while you have brainstorming sessions or team meetings, but can't get people to speak up? Well, before you try to bring about a change in them, change yourself.

The next time someone is talking or presenting their views, listen to them talk. Do not multitask when they talk. However tempting it may be, do not unlock your phone, check the time or stare at the other people who are listening in order to gauge their reaction to what is being said.

Rather, give your undivided attention to the person who is speaking, by turning your face and your entire upper body in the direction of the speaker. Try to make eye contact; it will boost the confidence of the speaker. Lean towards the speaker and nod every time they look towards you. In this way you indicate to the person that you are listening and understanding what they are trying to say.

It is extremely important to listen to people and also assure them that you are listening to what they have to say. When you do so, you are silently encouraging them to speak on. This will give them the confidence to speak up more and express their thoughts and ideas without hesitation!

3. Remove the barriers and encourage cooperation

Barriers have a very extremely negative impact on any attempts to collaborate and cooperate. So, when you sit down with your team, even for an informal chat, remove anything that forms a barrier between the rest of the team and you. Even if you are on an informal coffee break, make sure that you are not holding your coffee mug in a way that it forms a barrier between you and your team and looks like a deliberate effort to hinder communication.

A lot of the senior executives evaluate the comfort levels of every member of their team by observing how high they hold their coffee mugs while interacting with the rest of their team members or with the senior executives themselves. It has been observed that when an individual is uncomfortable with the situation, he or she tends to hold the mug higher, almost in level with their face. Individuals who hold their coffee mugs at their waist level tend to be more comfortable with their surroundings.

So, your holding of the coffee mug speaks volumes about your comfort level with your team, and you do not want to give off the impression that you are uncomfortable around them. When you show them that you are comfortable in your presence, you encourage them to collaborate with you and cooperate with you on projects without an ounce of hesitation.

So, ensure that whenever you speak to your team, both your lines of vision are clear with no barriers between you all.

4. Handshakes have a large impact on your connectivity with people

The most powerful and primitive nonverbal cue in the world is touch. When you touch someone, even for a very short period, on their hand, shoulder or arm, it creates a bond between you two, without even outing in a lot of effort.

While in a formal situation, touching informally is a very strict no-no. So how do you establish a bond with an individual without putting in a lot of effort?

A handshake is the easiest way to establish a warm bond in a workplace situation. This palpable contact ensures that there is an extremely positive and lasting impression on both parties involved in the handshake.

A study conducted by the Income Center for Trade Shows on handshakes has shown that when you shake hands with people, they are two times more likely to remember you, as opposed to people who you just orally interact with without any physical contact. The study also showed that when an individual shook hands with another, their interaction was friendlier and open, as opposed to an interaction between people who did not shake hands.

When you shake hands with a person, ensure that your handshake is firm and your palms are not sweaty. A limp handshake gives off an impression of being weak and nervous while an extremely firm handshake gives off an extremely wrong impression.

5. A simple smile can take you a long way

When you smile genuinely, it not only sparks feelings of happiness and well being in you, it also implies to the people around you that you are extremely cooperative, very trustworthy and can be approached without any sort of hesitation.

A genuine smile is one that creeps onto the face slowly, causes the face to light up, brings out crinkles near the eyes and is very slow to fade away. This smile is usually very distinguishable from the regular fake smiles.

Smiling has an extremely large impact on how people respond to you as an individual. Usually when you smile at someone, they will more often than not smile back. Our facial expressions have a way to trigger the emotions in ourselves, so when you make a person smile, you encourage feelings of positivity in the person for you.

So, even if you come face to face with a junior, a colleague, or a senior, who you absolutely cannot stand or do not wish to interact with, give them a heartfelt smile. They will respond to your smile, and this will help change their negative feelings for you into positive feelings, making it easier for you to interact and cooperate with them, without any hesitation.

6. Mirroring and mimicking expressions and postures can show agreement

Mirroring or mimicking of positions is a sure shot sign of agreement. The next time you are in a meeting try changing your posture. Maybe place your right elbow on the table and place your palm under your chin. Or grab a pencil with your left hand. Do you notice anyone changing their position so that their position mimics your position?

This shows that that particular individual is in agreement with your statements and that is their way of projecting their feelings to you. Similarly, even you mirror the position of the other person when you are in agreement with the sentiments of the individual.

The mirroring of positions is an extremely important part of creating a rapport between people and developing feelings of a bond.

Mirroring begins by a close observation of the person and recording the facial expression and bodily posture of the individual. Then, you subtly change your position so that your facial expressions are mimicking the facial expressions of the individual in concern and taking up the body posture of the individual too. When you do so, you help make the other person feel accepted in the particular situation and make them feel understood.

7. Animated hands help improve your speech

Brain imaging tests have shown that there is a region known as the Broca's area in our brain. The Broca's area is very important for speech production. This area is not only active when we are speaking, but also activates when we move our hands around. This is why the gesture of continually moving hands is commonly linked to our speech. When we gesture and move our hands around when we speak, we are actually providing power to our thinking.

Whenever people move their hands around and gesture using their hands, there is a considerable and noticeable improvement in their speech. If you feel unsure about this, try this trick and you will see that there is a considerable difference in your speech.

Stand in front of the mirror and recite something from memory with your arms by your sides. Notice your facial expressions and postures. Now, animate your hands while talking and notice the difference between your former positions and facial expressions and your present positions and facial expressions. You will notice that you speak with clearer thoughts and your sentences are tighter. Your language is more declarative and your sentences are more comprehensible.

8. If you want to get to know a person, observe the movement of their feet

When an individual tries to have complete control over their body language, they usually tend to try to control their facial expressions, gestures of the hands and arms, and the body postures. Usually the feet and legs always end up getting ignored and people never tend to control the response of their feet nor do they rehearse controlling their feet. Usually this is because the feet are safely tucked away under the table or are hidden behind a podium, or are generally not observed very closely.

So, if you want to know the truth about a person, especially if he or she tightly controls his or her facial emotions, body postures and hand or arm movements, observe his or her feet. When under stress or nervous, people will usually show their anxiety and nervousness by moving their feet around. They will shuffle their feet, fidget with them, and cross and uncross them repeatedly around each other or around pieces of furniture. They will stretch and curl their feet in order to relieve the tension in them and even kick jerkily in an attempt to escape from the uncomfortable or stressful situation that they are in.

According to a study, observers found that they could judge the emotions of the individual better by observing their entire body from head to toe, as opposed to just observing the upper body of the individual. You never know, even you may have been giving away a lot of your innermost feelings just by the movement of your feet.

9. If you wish to sound authoritative, do not raise your voice

Often people assume that the louder they speak, the higher the authority they portray. This is not true; rather it is the opposite! If you want to sound powerful and authoritative, make sure that you do not speak too loudly.

Before you go you on the dais to give a speech or make an extremely important phone call, make sure that your voice is at its regular pitch. The quickest way to do so is to do this little exercise before going off to give a speech or make that important phone call. Join your lips together, but make sure that you do not press them between your teeth, just simply join them. Slowly and repeatedly make this sound, "um hum, um hum, um hum, um hum, um, hum". Repeat this about four times. Your voice will get to its optimal pitch.

If you are woman, ensure that your voice does not go up when you end a sentence, while asking someone a question or are asking someone for his or her approval. Rather, when you are speaking your opinion, use the bureaucratic arc. In this, your statement begins on your regular pitch and slowly your pitch rises through the sentence and drops back to the normal pitch at the end of the statement.

Doing so makes you sound authoritative and powerful, without you having to raise your voice or repeatedly speak about your authority.

10. Uncrossed arms and legs help in increasing your memory power

Allan Pease and Barbara Pease, who are body language researchers, have reported an extremely fascinating and compelling find from their various researchers. According to them, the group of volunteers who attended a lecture and sat there with their arms and legs uncrossed remembered 38% more content of the lecture, as opposed to the group of volunteers that sat in the lecture with crossed arms and legs.

So, if you want to improve your retention prowess and your memory powers, always sit with your arms and legs uncrossed.

This will aid in increasing your retention capabilities and make you even more productive.

Also, if you observe that the people in your audience exhibit a defensive body language, like crossing their arms and legs and looking distracted overall, make sure you change your tactics. Break up for some coffee or suggest that everyone stand up and stretch for a few minutes or ask everyone to change his or her seating positions. Make sure that you do not resume your speech until their body language shows that they are open to you.

Following these aforementioned tips will ensure that the non-verbal impact that you have on your juniors, colleagues and seniors at your work place is increased tenfold and will aid you to become even more communicative and efficient quite effortlessly.

Chapter 9: Ten Tips On How To Use Non Verbal Communication To Your Advantage

1. Keep a keen eye on the non-verbal signals people give out

As established, people use a variety of ways to communicate with each other. Verbal communication is not the only communication people use. So, keep a very precise eye on little things like little gestures, the body posture, the little movements, tone and pitch of the voice, and eye contact. All these indicators can provide massive amounts of information, which usually is not put into words.

When you pay close attention to the little things people do without paying conscious attention to, you will end up understanding the minute details related to non-verbal communication. This will help you improve your own non-verbal communication skills.

2. Look for discrepancies in the way people behave

If an individual's words and his or her non-verbal behavior do not match together, you should pay extremely close attention that particular individual. For example, an individual may tell you that they are sad, but you may notice a weird twinkle in their eyes that denotes happiness.

A lot of researches have shown that when a person's words and their non verbal signs do not match, the person who is receiving the information will ignore what has been spoken and will focus more on the unspoken words that are "spoken" through the subconscious or unconscious behavior. This is the impact non-verbal communication has on the mind.

3. Pay attention to the tone of your voice and the pitch while you speak

Yes, this point has been mentioned earlier, but this point cannot be stressed upon enough. The tone of your voice can give away a lot of information, without you having to explicitly state each and every word. The tone of your voice can easily convey happiness, sadness, interest, disinterest, enthusiasm or the lack of it, anger, and a whole lot of emotions quite easily.

Take note of how the variation in the tones of your voice affect the people around you and how do they respond to that particular tone. Try to use the tone that emphasizes the emotions you want to communicate the most.

For example, if you wish to show a person that you are enthusiastic about a particular thing, try to introduce enthusiasm in your tone and take on a very animated and happy tone of voice.

4. Good eye contact is the key to better communication

As mentioned before, proper eye contact is very important. When you shy away from maintaining steady eye contact, you imply that you are hiding something or are trying to evade particular topic. While, if you maintain a very steady eye contact, you may come off as confrontational or as a liar or even come off as an extremely intimidating individual.

Yes, maintaining eye contact is an important aspect of communication, but you should understand that a good eye contact does not necessarily mean that you should creepily keep staring into the eyes of the person.

As a rule of thumb, eye contact should be no less than 4 seconds long or more than 5 seconds long. Anything less than 4 seconds is considered as shifty behavior, and anything more than 5 seconds is considered too creepy!

5. Ask plenty of questions about their body language signals

If you are in doubt or cannot make out a person's non-verbal signals, do not hesitate before asking a question. It is better to clarify things than get a wrong interpretation because you misinterpreted or misunderstood a part of the conversation.

The easiest way to do so is by asking for a direct clarification. Do not go in circles or try to hint at the question. Just directly approach the person and ask them. A good example would be to begin your question with the words, "so, are you saying that..."followed by your interpretation. If it is correct they will nod on and if your interpretation is incorrect, they will clarify it for you.

6. Use non-verbal signals in order to communicate more effectively

Verbal communication and non-verbal communication go hand in hand and aid you to easily put forth your thoughts. You can boost your communication prowess by using non-verbal communication that helps fortify and support your verbal statements.

This is extremely important while presenting an idea or thought, or while talking to a large group of people. Your minor body signals can help in reinforcing the idea in the minds of the audience members and helps them to understand the concept better.

7. Group the signals together in order to interpret them accurately

A small gesture can mean a lot of things or nothing at all. The most important part of interpreting non-verbal signals with precision is to look for a bunch of similar signals that imply a common thing.

If you concentrate too much on a single signal, you may end up getting the wrong impression of the person and about what the person is trying to tell you. For example, if the person is blinking too much, do not draw a conclusion that he or she is lying. If the blinking is combined with a lack of eye contact and staring at the floor, then the person is lying is an acceptable conclusion.

8. Keep the situation in mind before drawing the conclusion

When you are trying to communicate with other people, keep the context the conversation occurs in and the situation in mind. There are a lot of situations that require you to behave in an extremely formal manner, and this formal behavior may be interpreted in a variety of ways in various other situations.

Always consider the situation and based on that decide if a non-verbal communication is apt for the situation or not. While trying to master non-verbal communication, always practice on how to use non-verbal signals in a variety of formal situations that have varying levels of formality required.

9. Keep in mind that your signs can be misread or misinterpreted

Some people believe that a firm handshake is the sign of a strong personality who is very confident about him or herself, while a limp handshake is an indication of a weak personality who is extremely nervous.

While this holds true for most people, sometimes a limp handshake may be due to a disease like arthritis. So, what may be construed to be a weak personality may be a disease!

This is why looking for groups of non-verbal signals is extremely important and this is exactly why you should judge people based on the groups of their non-verbal behavioral traits rather than a single observed trait.

10. Practice makes man (and woman) perfect

A lot of people have just the knack to interpret non-verbal signals perfectly, and even use them quite effortlessly without putting in a lot of effort from their end. These people are commonly described to have the talent of "reading people".

Well, for all those of us who are not born with this skill, this skill is quite achievable if you only practice. Pay attention to what everyone says and does. Make notes and compare the commonly observed signs and their implied meanings. By noting other people's behavior only can one improve their own non-verbal skills.

In order to practice your non-verbal reading skills do the following exercise:

Head to a nearby coffee house, grab a coffee and prop open your notebook. Now just sit and observe people; make note of their posture, expressions, how they carry themselves, how the place their limbs, etc. in your notebook. Try and draw conclusions for each sign you note down. Slowly and steadily you will learn how to correctly read the signs and draw the perfect conclusions for the same.

Bonus Chapter: Sign Language

Sign language is a type of gesture language that is used by people who cannot speak or hear. It is also used by people who cannot speak a foreign tongue and need to communicate with the locals. Sign language can also be used by students who wish to communicate mid class and do not want to be caught passing notes.

There are a few standard acceptable sign language gestures that you can learn and communicate with a person who cannot hear or what you can use when you find yourself in a foreign land who do not speak your tongue.

How are you?

How is performed by placing bent fingers adjacent to each other and the thumbs sticking upwards. It is performed by pointing to the person.

I am fine

'I' is performed by placing index finger on the chest and "fine" is performed by placing the thumb on the chest and the rest of the fingers spread out.

Please

The word "please" is indicated by placing your right palm on your chest and rotating it clockwise (from the view of the observer) a few times.

Store

To indicate the word "store" life both your hands and bend them at the wrist, with your fingers pointing downwards. Move your fingers away from your body twice in quick succession.

Pizza

There are various signs used to portray the word "pizza", but the one that we have mentioned here is the most commonly used one. Hold your right hand in such a way that all your fingers are pointing towards you and your palm faces upwards. Lightly bend your entire finger in order to make a large "spoon like" structure and hold it a few inches away from your mouth. Slowly bring it closer to your mouth and take it away. Repeat this a few times.

Hungry

To indicate hunger, form a "C" like shape with your right hand and place it horizontally on your chest with your fingers and thumb touching your chest. Move your hand up and down a few times.

Signs for relatives

Mother

Mother is signaled by placing the thumb on your chin with the palm facing outwards and fingers spread out.

Father

Father is signaled by placing the thumb on the forehead with the palm facing to the side.

Baby

Baby is signaled by crossing hands and swaying it left to right.

Other Gestures

Hurt

To signal hurt, you have to close all fingers but the index finger of both hands and point them towards each other. You can also make a crying face to accentuate the hurt.

Cat

A cat is signaled by using the thumb and index finger to pinch an imaginary whisker while the rest of the fingers spread out.

Dog

To signal a dog you can simply snap your finger twice.

Dollar

To signal dollars, you have to hold your left hand in front of you and cup the tips of your left fingers with your right hand. You must then slide your right hand away from the left while keeping the left stationary.

Cost

To ask the cost of something, you must place your non-writing hand in front of you and draw an "X" with the back of your writing hand.

Please

You can signal please by placing your right hand, palm facing inwards over your heart and making a circling motion.

Thank you

You can signal thank you by placing the fingers of your dominant hand over your lips and slowly moving it forward in the direction of the receiver.

Help

To signal help, you can spread out the left hand in front of you and place the right over it after clenching it with the thumb sticking upwards.

Day

To signal day, place your non-dominant arm across your chest with the palm down. Place the elbow of your dominant arm on the back of your non-dominant arm's hand. Slowly trace an arc down to the elbow of your non-dominant arm and rest it there.

Night

To indicate night place your non-dominant hand with its palm facing downwards and the fingertips pointing to the side. Place the wrist of your dominant hand on the thumb of your non dominant hand and place your entire palm on the back of your hand with your finger tips pointing downwards.

Dollar or dollars

To signal the word dollar or dollars, hold your left hand with the palm facing towards you and the fingers pointing to the right. Grab the fingers on your left hand using your right hand and slowly slide the fingers of your right hand off the fingers of your left hand.

Conclusion

It will be wise to remember that all the different body language traits mentioned in this book may or may not apply to every individual. Something that you may find applicable to a particular individual in a specific situation may not apply to another individual in the very same situation!

Therefore, it is very important that you study the normal behavior of the individual for a while before actually trying to interpret their body signals. A lot of times what you may take to be a sign may be a force of habit for that particular individual. For example, you may think that when the person is blinking too much, he may be a liar, but over time you may observe that naturally he is a fast blinker and blinks fast in each and every situation!

This book aimed at unraveling the complexities of body language and how you can interpret it better. I hope to have succeeded in at least building a little curiosity in you and prompting you to further explore the mysteries of the science of body language.

You May Enjoy Jeffery's Other Books

Author Page

hyperurl.co/Jeffdawson

PSYCHOPATH: Manipulation, Con Men And Relationship Fraud

smarturl.it/psychoa

Boundaries: Line Between Right And Wrong

hyperurl.co/boundaries

Personality Disorders: Histrionic and Borderline Personality Disorders Unmasked

hyperurl.co/borderline

BODY LANGUAGE: How To Spot A Liar And Communicate Clearly

hyperurl.co/bodylang

Alpha Male: Be A Real Man And Squash The Competition

smarturl.it/alphamale

MIND CONTROL:

Manipulation, Deception and Persuasion Exposed

hyperurl.co/mindcontrol

Tantric Sex and What Women Want - Box Set Collection: Couples Communication and Pleasure Guide

hyperurl.co/sexwomenwant